Learn to Cook

Starters

Learn to Cook

Starters

Anne Chapman

HARLAXTON

The plate of Crudité, (p. 11), on page two has a bowl of Taramasalata, (p. 10) and Mayonnaise, (p. 12), to dip the salad vegetables into. The preparation for the crudité is shown on the front and back endpapers. The salad vegetables look just as inviting before they were assembled.

Published by
Harlaxton Publishing Limited
2 Avenue Road, Grantham, Lincolnshire, NG31 6TA
United Kingdom
A Member of the Weldon International Group of Companies

First Published in 1994

© Copyright 1994 Harlaxton Publishing Limited
© Copyright 1994 Design Harlaxton Publishing Limited

Publisher: Robin Burgess
Project Coordinator: Barbara Beckett
Designer: Rachel Rush
Editor: Alison Leach
Illustrator: Kate Finnie
Jacket photographer: Rodney Weidland
Inside photography: Andrew Elton
Food stylist: Janet Marsh Lillie
Produced by Barbara Beckett Publishing
Colour Separation: G.A. Graphics, Stamford, UK
Printer: Imago, Singapore

British Library Cataloguing-in-Publication data.
A catalogue record for this book is available from the British Library

Title: Learn to Cook, STARTERS
ISBN: 1 85837 078 7

Learn to Cook

Contents

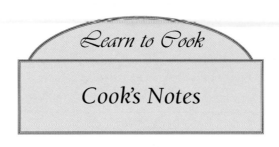

Cook's Notes

Measurements

As the metric/imperial/US equivalents given are not exact, follow only one system of measurement within the recipe. All spoon and cup measurements are level. Standard spoon and cup measures are used in all the recipes. I recommend using a graduated nest of measuring cups: 1 cup, ½ cup, ⅓ cup and ¼ cup. The graduated nest of spoons comprises 1 tablespoon, 1 teaspoon, ½ teaspoon and ¼ teaspoon. For liquids, use a standard litre or imperial pint measuring jug, which also shows cup measurements. A

Ovens should be preheated to the specified temperature. The heat on top of the hob (stove top) should be set at medium unless otherwise stated.

Ingredients

Fresh fruit and vegetables should be used in the recipes unless otherwise stated. **Herb** quantities are for fresh herbs; if fresh are unobtainable, use half the quantity of dried herbs. Use freshly ground black **pepper** whenever pepper is listed; use **salt** and pepper to individual taste. Use plain (all-purpose) **flour** unless otherwise stated. Fresh **ginger** should be used throughout, unless ground ginger is called for. Use fresh **chillies**; if substituting dried chillies, halve the quantity. Cold-pressed virgin olive **oil** is recommended, but any type may be used. Use unsalted **butter**. Preferably use fermented wine **vinegar**; however, cider vinegar and malt vinegar may be substituted if preferred. White granulated **sugar** is used unless stated otherwise.

Broad Bean Eggah, (p. 40) is an omelette-like cake eaten throughout the Middle East. Eat hot or cold as a starter to an alfresco meal.

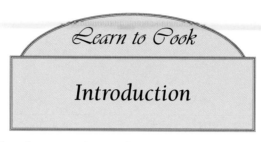

Learn to Cook

Introduction

The start of a lunch or dinner sets the tone for the rest of the meal. Even the fact that you are serving a starter means this is a special meal, thoughtfully planned. Usually I choose the starter after I have decided on the main course. If it is a rich, savoury dish like a beef casserole, I will choose something light to start with, such as Parma Ham with Melon (p. 20), Asparagus with Vinaigrette (p. 23), a wedge of Smoked Fish Flan (p. 47) or a Spinach Salad (p. 16). If you are planning a simple main course like French roast chicken, you can lash out with more complex flavours as a starter—a Seafood Pasta (p.20), slices of Pork and Veal Terrine (p. 32) with cornichons (gherkins), an Onion Omelette (p. 39) or Smoked Salmon Crêpes (p. 44).

Many of these starters can be eaten very casually, not necessarily at the dinner table. The dips and crudités can be passed around on a large plate while you chat and enjoy a drink. Most of these starters can also be used as a main course for a light lunch or supper.

This book will teach you the basic step-by-step method of making dips, sauces and salads, as well as how to create your own ideas. It shows you how to make fresh pasta, pâtés and terrines. There are simple hints to make a perfect French omelette and crêpes and how to make short-crust pastry (basic pie dough).

The instructions are clearly set out, and many of the recipes are photographed in preparation stages to show a special technique as well as what the finished dish looks like and how to present it for the table. Detailed step-by-step line drawings illustrate techniques such as how to hold the omelette pan and swirl it to get a thin, even omelette. There are boxes of handy hints and information on such matters as how to cook hard-boiled eggs, how to julienne vegetables and the absorption method of cooking rice. Every cooking technique required in these recipes is included and explained.

The recipes are cross-referenced within the book. For example, there are dips that can also be used for pasta sauces or to fill an omelette or crêpe. Enjoy experimenting once you have mastered some of the techniques.

A glossary of cooking terms is on the last page for you to look up any term that is unfamiliar. There is a list of recipes on page 5 for your reference. Be sure to read the information on measurements and ingredients on page 6.

One of the most important things to do when trying a new recipe is to read the recipe very thoroughly before starting. Check that you have all the ingredients, and make an estimate of the amount of time needed. Have you time to make fresh pasta and a sauce? Or would it be better just to make one item fresh?

The recipes are drawn from cuisines round the world such as Italy, France, the Middle East, Germany and Mexico.

No special equipment is needed for these dishes, though I would recommend having a heavy, cast-iron frying pan (skillet) just for omelettes and another for crêpes. You will need a porcelain

Hummus bi Tahina, (p. 11), is an easily made dip from chickpeas, left and sesame paste, second from right. Soak the chickpeas overnight before cooking.

flan dish or a loose-bottomed flan tin (pie pan). It is worthwhile investing in an attractive terrine dish, which will decorate the table besides being practical for cooking. Saucepans and frying pans are far more efficient if they have heavy metal bases and tight-fitting lids because the thick base ensures even cooking and retention of heat. A food processor is a worthwhile acquisition if you are serious about cooking, because it saves so much time and energy.

Buy your fruit and vegetables seasonally and they will be cheaper and fresher if you are a canny shopper. Store salad vegetables unwashed in polythene bags left open for the air to circulate. Green polythene bags are available now which will prolong the life of the vegetables in the refrigerator.

I hope you enjoy making these recipes and eating the delicious results with your family and friends.

Bon appétit!

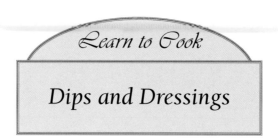

Learn to Cook

Dips and Dressings

Guacamole from Mexico, aïoli from Provence, taramasalata from Greece and hummus from the Middle East—all are dips to enjoy at the start of a meal or with pre-dinner drinks. Generally the dip is scooped up with pieces of bread, toast, grissini or corn chips. Vegetable pieces are even tastier and more nutritious, so try celery stalks, small tomatoes, bean sprouts, fennel, mangetout (snow peas), mushrooms, cos (romaine) lettuce leaves, sticks of carrot, beetroot, cucumber, asparagus, pepper (capsicum, bell pepper), and courgette (baby marrow, zucchini), whole radishes with a little green left on, florets of cauliflower and broccoli, and fresh beans or spring onions (scallions). Fruit wedges make a refreshing change; apple, pear, avocado, pineapple or melon are delicious. Dip the apple and pear in a solution of half lemon juice and half water as soon as they are cut to prevent them from browning. Small cocktail sausages or thin Italian sausage and any cold seafood add a touch of luxury to the idea of the dip. You can serve a selection of these small edibles, together with the dip, on individual plates. For example, some cooked prawns, radishes, celery sticks, a wedge of lemon and a scoop of aïoli will make a splendid start to a special meal.

All these dips are very simple and quick to make, as well as nutritious.

Guacamole

1 avocado, peeled and chopped
1 onion, finely chopped
2 tablespoons soured cream or plain yoghurt

1 tablespoon lemon juice
¼ teaspoon chilli powder

Put all the ingredients except the chilli into a food processor and blend well. Spoon into a bowl and sprinkle with the chilli powder.
Serves 4

Taramasalata

175 g/6 oz smoked cod's roe paste
60 g/2 oz/1 cup fresh breadcrumbs
2 garlic cloves, crushed

5 tablespoons olive oil
2 tablespoons lemon juice
4 lemon wedges to garnish

Put all the ingredients into a food processor and blend well. Spoon into a flat bowl and serve with lemon wedges and crusty bread.
Serves 4-6

Smoked Trout Dip

Serve this dip with hot toast fingers and sticks of celery.

1 smoked trout, about 300 g (11 oz)
250 ml/8 fl oz/1 cup soured cream
200 g/7 oz/1 cup cottage cheese

2 tablespoons lemon juice
1 tablespoon chopped chives
½ teaspoon pepper

Remove the skin from the trout and carefully lift all the flesh from the bones and flake it into a food processor. Add the rest of the ingredients and blend to a smooth paste. Spoon into a bowl and chill for several hours before serving.
Serves 4-6

Hummus bi Tahina

150 g/5 oz/1 cup chickpeas (garbanzo beans),
   soaked
4 tablespoons tahina
Juice of 2 lemons
4 garlic cloves, crushed

1 teaspoon salt
2 tablespoons olive oil
1 teaspoon cumin seeds
1 teaspoon paprika
Parsley sprigs, to garnish

Cook the chickpeas (garbanzo beans) in fresh water for about 1¼ hours or until tender, drain. Put all the ingredients except paprika and parsley into a food processor. Blend to a creamy paste. Serve on a plate dusted with paprika and garnished with parsley.
Serves 4-6.

Crudités

'Crudités' simply mean a plate of fresh raw vegetables, usually served in France with a vinaigrette (p. 13) or aïoli. The plate is passed around so that each person can make a selection. It is easy to present an attractive combination. Choose from the vegetables mentioned in the introduction (p. 8). Hard-boiled eggs (this page) make a tasty addition, as do small cooked potatoes and strips of red cabbage.

Hard-boiled Eggs *A simple cooking method very often mishandled—if the eggs are cooked too long, they will toughen and taste unpleasant. The eggs to be cooked should be at room temperature. Bring a saucepan of water to the boil, put in the eggs and boil them for 8 minutes, then plunge them into cold water to make them easier to peel.*

Mayonnaise

2 egg yolks
1 teaspoon French mustard
¼ teaspoon salt

250 ml/8 fl oz/1 cup olive oil
1 tablespoon lemon juice

Beat together the egg yolks, mustard and salt. Add the oil, drop by drop, beating continuously. You can use a whisk, an electric beater or a food processor. As the mayonnaise thickens, you can add the oil in larger quantities. When thick, add the lemon juice and stir in with a wooden spoon. You may need to add more lemon juice or hot water after the mayonnaise has been stored for a while, as it will thicken up again.

Makes 250 ml/8 fl oz/1 cup

Aïoli. *Made in exactly the same way as mayonnaise, but use 6 fat garlic cloves, crushed in the salt, instead of the mustard.*

Mayonnaise

| Beat the egg yolks, mustard and salt together. | Add the oil, drop by drop, beating continuously until it has thickened. | Squeeze some lemon juice. | Add the lemon juice to whiten and bring the mayonnaise to the desired consistency. |

  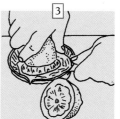 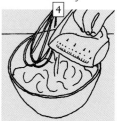

Herby Yoghurt Dip

A refreshing dip to serve in summer. Pitta bread or crusty bread and raw vegetables go very well with it.

250 ml/8 fl oz/1 cup plain yoghurt
200 g/7 oz/1 cup cottage cheese
15 g/1½ oz/¼ cup finely chopped coriander (cilantro) or mint leaves
15 g/1½ oz/¼ cup finely chopped parsley

3 garlic cloves, finely chopped
1 tablespoon lemon juice
1 tablespoon French mustard
1 teaspoon pepper
½ teaspoon salt

Put all the ingredients into a food processor and blend to a thick, smooth paste. Add more lemon juice if necessary.

Serves 6

Rosemary vinegar, extra virgin olive oil, French mustard and pepper ready to make a classic Vinaigrette to flavour salads and vegetables.

Vinaigrette (French Salad Dressing)

I add lots of herbs when making vinaigrette to use with crudités, but not necessarily when dressing other dishes. Use your imagination about whether they are needed or not. Experiment with different oils–walnut and hazelnut, for example. Try sherry or champagne vinegar. Add green peppercorns, shallots, chilli and soy sauce for a change.

4 tablespoons extra virgin olive oil
1 tablespoon wine vinegar
4 teaspoons French mustard

1 teaspoon pepper
1 tablespoon chopped chives
1 tablespoon chopped parsley

Combine all the ingredients in a screw-topped jar and shake vigorously. Store in the coldest part of the refrigerator to help emulsify the dressing.

Serves 6

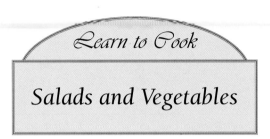

Learn to Cook

Salads and Vegetables

Increasingly we are discovering how good vegetables and salads are for us and what fascinating dishes they can be in their own right—not just as an accompaniment to meat or seafood. Many varieties of vegetables and salad leaves are readily available these days, so when you are shopping always choose the youngest and freshest. If they are in season, they should not be too expensive. Examine them for flaws and feel them for ripeness.

Never overcook vegetables especially if they are to be eaten in salads or as a starter on their own. They should be *al dente*, that is, firm to the bite and slightly crunchy.

When boiling vegetables, place potatoes, carrots and other root vegetables in cold water and bring to the boil. Other vegetables should be put into boiling water.

Some vegetables for salads are simply blanched first—that is, they are immersed in boiling water for a minute, drained and put under a running cold tap to cool down. Blanch green beans, cauliflower, broccoli and cabbage.

Please yourself whether you peel potatoes and root vegetables. They look better peeled but nowadays we know that most of the valuable fibre and many minerals are in the skin or just

Salad leaves should be washed thoroughly, drained and dried in a salad dryer or in a fresh tea-towel.

beneath it, so it seems a shame to lose them. Peel them just before cooking so they don't discolour.

Nearly all vegetables can be made into a salad or be part of a mixed salad dip (p. 10). Salad leaves include cabbage, the different varieties of lettuce, endive, watercress, curly endive (witloof), chicory, spinach, radicchio, rocket (arugula) and any number of herbs.

Salad leaves should be fresh and not wilted. Store them whole in the refrigerator and wash them just before using. Choose only the best-looking leaves. Wash them well and drain. Dry them either with a tea-towel (dish cloth) or in a salad dryer. If the leaves are not dry, the salad dressing won't stick to the leaves—you'll just have a soggy mess. You can return the washed and dried leaves to the refrigerator until ready to eat. Add the vinaigrette just before serving, and toss the leaves gently in front of the guests.

Other ingredients to add to a salad are pitted olives, cheese, anchovies, bread, croutons, nuts, pieces of cooked meat and seafood. Fruits can be splendid too—grapes, pineapple, orange, apple, pear, melon, papaya (pawpaw) and berries.

If you haven't made salads before, follow the directions for the salads in this chapter. When you are feeling confident, make selections from the vegetables, salad leaves and other ingredients and compose your own salads. It is always exciting to invent a new salad. Experiment with your vinaigrette as well. Always keep eye appeal in mind when composing or deciding how to cut a vegetable – should the cucumber be in thin long strips or slices? Do not tear the large lettuce leaves up too small, and never cut them. Consider the textures and colours of the leaves. You can get wonderful dramatic effects such as black olives and baby beetroots (beets) nestling amongst dark watercress and spinach.

How to cut up Vegetables. *It is worthwhile spending some time teaching yourself how to cut up vegetables the professional way. The technique is used for julienning—cutting food into short, thin strips—and for shredding vegetables such as cabbage. It is a very practical and fast technique that will make parts of a food processor redundant.*

Holding a knife the correct way

Your wrist should be relaxed and your knife very sharp.	*Raise the handle just high enough to move it up and down easily.*	*Never lift the point of the knife from the cutting board, as it is like a pivot.*	*Your left fore-finger and middle finger guide the knife, and the left hand retreats as the cutting continues.*

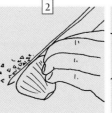

Salad Variations

Spinach Salad. Spinach leaves, chopped hard-boiled eggs, croûtons, pine nuts and hot pieces of bite-size bacon tossed with a herbed vinaigrette.

Beef Salad. Warm slices of rare beef tossed through lettuce and watercress with chopped walnuts and a vinaigrette made with walnut oil.

Prawn (Shrimp) Salad. Cos (romaine) lettuce with cooked, peeled prawns (shrimp) and a julienne of carrots and celery tossed with a dill-flavoured vinaigrette.

Green Salad with Violets. A mixture of salad leaves—whatever is available—with violets tossed over the leaves just before serving.

Croûtons. *Croûtons are small cubes of bread which have been fried in oil or butter until crisp and golden. Use them as a garnish in salads and with omelettes as well as in soup. Add a few garlic cloves to the pan to make garlic croûtons for a change. Cut the bread from a stale white loaf. Brush with oil and grill (broil) or bake in the oven to dry them out.*

Salade Niçoise

A favourite salad from the south of France, Salade Niçoise can be a starter or a light lunch.

Lettuce leaves, washed and dried	185 g/6½ oz canned tuna
3 potatoes, cooked and quartered	2 hard-boiled eggs, quartered
3 tomatoes, quartered	12 black olives, pitted
250 g/9 oz green beans, blanched	6 anchovy fillets, drained
½ cucumber, sliced	Vinaigrette (p. 13)

Assemble all the ingredients in a large salad bowl in the order they are listed. Dress the salad with the vinaigrette at the table just before serving.
Serves 6

A classic combination of favourite ingredients from the south of France make up this delectable bowl of Salad Niçoise. Composing a salad like this is relaxing and gratifying to our senses of smell and sight as well as taste. The famous opera composer, Rossini, believed a salad maker is born, not made.

Assembling Greek Country Salad

Remove the core and seeds from the pepper (capsicum, bell pepper) and cut into thin rings.

Cut the tomatoes into wedges.

Chop the parsley.

Assemble all the ingredients in the salad bowl and toss the vinaigrette through gently.

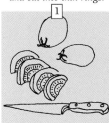

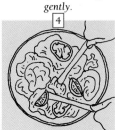

Greek Country Salad

A hearty salad for summer eating. The fresh salty taste of the feta cheese, olives and capers enlivens the dish.

1 lettuce, washed and dried

3 tomatoes, quartered

1 green pepper (capsicum, bell pepper),
   cut into thin rings

1 cucumber, cut into finger-length sticks

10 spring onions (scallions), thinly sliced

225 g/8 oz feta cheese, cut into small cubes

18 black olives, pitted

1 tablespoon capers

60g/2 oz/1 cup parsley, chopped

Vinaigrette (p. 13), made with oregano,
   omit mustard

Assemble all the ingredients in a large wide salad bowl. Add the vinaigrette just before serving.
Serves 6

Panzanella

This is an Italian salad that can be a light lunch or a starter. The most important thing is to use a good-tasting, firm and coarse-textured bread.

450 g/1 lb stale white bread, thickly sliced

½ cucumber, sliced

6 spring onions (scallions), sliced

30g/1 oz/½ cup basil leaves

6 tomatoes, quartered

Vinaigrette (p. 13), omit mustard

Tear the bread into large bite-size pieces and sprinkle with a little water. Squeeze gently to remove moisture and keep in the refrigerator for several hours. Put all the other ingredients except the vinaigrette into a salad bowl. Lay the bread on top and dress at the table.
Serves 6

Waldorf Coleslaw

If low-fat yoghurt is used in the dressing, this makes a splendid salad for those watching their weight.

½ cabbage, shredded
2 celery sticks, sliced
1 apple, chopped
4 spring onions (scallions), sliced
90 g/3 oz/½ cup sultanas (golden raisins)

Vinaigrette (p. 13)
3 tablespoons mayonnaise (p. 12)
3 tablespoons soured cream or low–fat yoghurt
60 g/2 oz/½ cup walnuts, chopped

Put the cabbage, celery, apple, spring onions and sultanas in a salad bowl. Toss the vinaigrette through and chill until needed. Just before serving, mix the mayonnaise, soured cream and walnuts together and mix through the salad.
Serves 6

German Potato Salad

A salad much beloved at picnics and barbecues–there is never any left! The potato tastes much better cut in slices than in cubes.

6 potatoes
6 spring onions (scallions), chopped
350 ml/12 fl oz/1½ cups chicken stock (broth)

4 tablespoons white wine vinegar
250 ml/8 fl oz/1 cup mayonnaise (p. 12)
2 tablespoons chopped dill or parsley, to garnish

These sliced potatoes for German Potato Salad have already been marinated in stock and vinegar and are being coated with mayonnaise.

Boil the potatoes in their skins until almost cooked. Drain and peel them while they are still hot and cut them into slices. Put them into a bowl with the spring onions. Put the stock and vinegar into a saucepan and bring to the boil. Pour the hot liquid over the potatoes and stir gently to ensure it has covered all the slices. Leave to marinate for 30 minutes. If there is liquid left, pour it off. Fold in the mayonnaise and coat the potatoes thoroughly. Garnish with dill or parsley.
Serves 6-8

Tomato and Mozzarella Salad

Another salad from Italy–simply made and delicious, especially if you use the finest quality oil and have sun-ripened tomatoes. Try it also with feta cheese which has been marinated in olive oil for several days in the refrigerator.

4 tomatoes, sliced
2 mozzarella cheeses, sliced
Salt and pepper

5 tablespoons cold-pressed virgin olive oil
30 g/1 oz/½ cup basil leaves, to garnish

Arrange the tomato slices on 4 plates and place the mozzarella slices on top. Sprinkle with salt and pepper and the oil. Garnish with the basil leaves.
Serves 4

Storing Tomatoes. *Tomatoes should not be kept in the refrigerator. They will ripen left out of the refrigerator and have much more flavour than when they have been chilled. If you have large quantities, turn some of the ripe ones into a purée and store it in the refrigerator or freezer. Plunge the tomatoes into boiling water just long enough to loosen their skins, then peel them, chop them coarsely and purée them in a food processor.*

Parma Ham with Melon

A very simple starter relying on fine quality ingredients. Finely sliced salami can be used instead of ham. Fresh ripe figs go wonderfully with this ham as well.

12 slices Parma ham (prosciutto)
1 ripe melon, cut into 12 wedges

1 teaspoon pepper
1 lemon, quartered, to garnish

Lay 3 slices of ham on each plate with 3 slices of melon. Sprinkle with pepper and garnish with a lemon wedge.
Serves 4

German Potato Salad, (p. 19), can be flavoured with mint as well as dill or parsley.

Vegetable Starters

Globe Artichokes. A favourite spring vegetable in many countries. Prepare the artichoke by cutting off the loose and tough outer leaves around the base. Snap off the stalk. Boil in water for 20 minutes and drain. Serve, one per person, with either vinaigrette (p. 13) or mayonnaise (p. 12). To eat, pull off one leaf at a time and dip the fleshy end into the sauce, then scrape off the tender base of the leaf between your teeth. When you get to the hairy choke, cut it out and eat the artichoke base. They can also be simply served with melted butter or they can be stuffed. Prepare the artichokes as in the illustration below and stuff them with a mixture of breadcrumbs and chopped herbs. Cover with a little stock and simmer for half an hour.

Preparing Globe Artichokes

Snap off the stalk.   *Cut the top leaves off.*   *Cut off tough outer leaves.*   *Take out the hairy choke.*

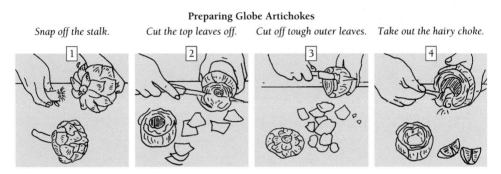

Asparagus. Asparagus needs to be cooked for only 6 minutes, so that it remains al dente, that is, still a little crisp, when eaten. Before cooking snap off the hard ends; the stalk will naturally break at the right place when bent. Discard the butt ends and put the tops into boiling water for 6 minutes, then drain and refresh. Serve with vinaigrette (p. 13) poured over immediately, with melted butter or with mayonnaise (p. 12). Add mixed herbs, such as parsley, chives and tarragon, to both sauces, if liked.

Leeks. Trim the tops off the leeks and cut a cross through the green ends. Plunge them into water to get rid of any grit clinging inside the leaves. Cook the leeks in boiling water for 15 minutes until tender; drain. Pour over a vinaigrette dressing (p. 13). Serve garnished with black olives. Try pouring some of the Herby Yoghurt Dip (p. 12) over for a change, and sprinkle with fresh herbs.

Fennel. Cut the bulb into bite-size pieces and proceed as for leeks above.

The fennel on this salad has been cooked, drained and dressed with vinaigrette and garnished with black olives.

Overleaf: Hummus bi Tahini, (p. 11), surrounded by tasty morsels to enjoy the dip with. All the ingredients can be ready in a few hours before the guests arrive saving you last minute preparations.

Stuffing tomatoes

Cut the top off the tomato and scoop out the pulp.

Mix the stuffing ingredients together in a bowl.

Spoon the stuffing into the tomato and replace the tomato top.

Put the tomatoes onto an oiled oven dish and pour the rest of the oil over.

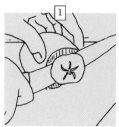  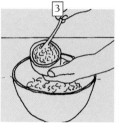 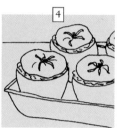

Stuffed Tomatoes

6 tomatoes
225g/8 oz/1½ cups cooked rice (p. 27)
2 garlic cloves, chopped
1 tablespoon drained capers
2 tablespoons chopped parsley

1½ tablespoons currants
1 teaspoon pepper
½ teaspoon nutmeg
175 ml/6 fl oz / ¾ cup olive oil

Carefully cut the top off each tomato. Hollow out the tomatoes and chop up the resulting pulp. Put the pulp in a bowl with the other ingredients except the oil. Add half the oil and mix well. Spoon the mixture into the tomatoes and put the caps back on. Put the tomatoes into an oiled ovenproof dish and pour the rest of the oil over. Cook in a preheated oven at 180°C/350°F/gas 4 for about 45 minutes or until soft.
Serves 6

Greek-style Mushrooms

3 tablespoons olive oil
2 shallots, chopped
200 ml/7 fl oz/¾ cup beef stock (broth)
150 ml/¼ pint/⅔ cup dry white wine
1 tablespoon lemon juice

2 garlic cloves, chopped
1 tablespoon tomato paste
1 teaspoon pepper
2 teaspoons coriander seeds
450 g/1 lb small mushrooms, wiped

Heat the oil in a saucepan and sauté the onion until softened. Add the remaining ingredients except the mushrooms. Bring the sauce to the boil and simmer for 10 minutes. Add the mushrooms and cook for 5 minutes or until tender. Remove them with a slotted spoon to a serving bowl. Reduce the sauce to about half and pour over the mushrooms.
Serves 6

Learn to Cook

Pasta

A traditional first course in Italy served with thousands of different sauces and over 50 shapes of pasta. Most sauces go well with both fresh and dried pasta.

Cook pasta in a large pot of rapidly boiling water until it *al dente*, that is soft but still a little firm. Fresh pasta will take 5–6 minutes to cook; dried pasta takes 15–20 minutes. Drain the pasta and put it into warm, wide soup plates or a large warmed bowl. Serve the sauce on top of the individual plates or mix it through if serving in a large bowl. Always serve with freshly grated Parmesan cheese unless it is a fish sauce. Guests help themselves to the cheese.

Bolognaise Sauce

Serve with freshly made pasta in warm bowls and garnish with grated Parmesan cheese.

2 tablespoons olive oil	½ teaspoon grated nutmeg
1 onion, finely chopped	1 tablespoon chopped oregano
1 celery stick, finely chopped	Salt and pepper
1 carrot, finely chopped	2 tablespoons tomato paste
200 g/7 oz/1½ cups minced (ground) beef	475 ml/16 fl oz/2 cups beef stock
200 g/7 oz /1½ cups minced (ground) pork	175 ml/6 fl oz/1¾ cup milk
125 ml/4 fl oz/½ cup dry white wine	60 g/2 oz/½ cup grated Parmesan cheese, to garnish

Heat the oil in a saucepan and add the onion, celery, and carrot. Sauté for 10 minutes. Add the beef and pork. Stir-fry for a few minutes until the meat changes colour, then add the wine. Season with the nutmeg, oregano, salt and pepper, then add the tomato paste and stock. Mix well and let the sauce simmer for an hour. Add the milk. When the milk has mostly evaporated, the sauce is ready.

Serves 6–8

Cooking Rice. *I believe the absorption method is the best way to cook rice. You need 1½ parts of water to 1 part of rice. Put both in a saucepan with plenty of room for the rice to expand. (One cup of uncooked rice becomes 3 cups when cooked.) Bring the water to the boil, stir once, lower the heat to simmer, and tightly close in the heat. The rice will be ready—al dente, or firm to the bite—in 20–25 minutes. Brown rice will take 10–15 minutes longer. Fluff up the cooked rice with a fork. The liquid will have been absorbed by the rice. Use chicken stock instead of water for a tasty change.*

Fresh Pasta

It's fun and rewarding to make your own pasta if you have time. With practice it doesn't take very long at all.

250 g/9 oz/2¼ cups flour, sifted
3 egg yolks
1 tablespoon olive oil

¼ teaspoon salt
4 tablespoons iced water
30 g/1 oz/2 tablespoons butter

Put the flour on a cold surface and make a well in the centre. Into it put the egg yolks, oil, salt and most of the water. Mix the centre items first, then gradually add the flour in from the sides. Keep mixing until you have a dough. Add more water if necessary. Work the dough with the palm of your hand until it is like an elastic ball and it no longer sticks to your fingers. Cover it with clingfilm (plastic wrap) and chill for 1 hour.

Sprinkle flour on your work surface and roll out the dough to a thickness of about 2 mm/ ¹⁄₁₆ inch. Now roll up the thin sheet of dough into a cylinder and cut slices off to the desired width of the pasta—1 cm/⅜ inch for a wide ribbon pasta, and finer as you gain confidence. Unroll the strips and hang them on racks to dry for an hour or two before cooking. Chill after drying if the pasta is not being cooked immediately.

Making fresh pasta

Make a well in the centre of the flour and put in the egg yolks, oil, salt and most of the water.	*After mixing the dough chill it. Roll it out thinly with a rolling pin.*	*Roll up the dough into a cylinder and slice evenly.*	*Hang and dry the pasta and then cook in rapidly boiling water for 5–6 minutes.*

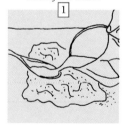 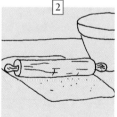 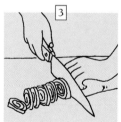 

Seafood Pasta Sauce

If you cannot get fresh mussels use 500 g/18 oz/1½ cups of fresh scallops instead.

1 kg/2¼ lb/1½ cups mussels in their shells
250 ml/8 fl oz/1 cup water
1 tablespoon olive oil
500 g/18 oz green (raw) prawns (shrimp)

125 ml/4 fl oz/½ cup white wine
250 ml/8 fl oz/1 cup tomato sauce (p. 30)
375 g/13 oz pasta
12 basil leaves, to garnish

The Seafood Pasta Sauce in this picture has been made with scallops as mussels were out of season.
They are served over saffron flavoured tagliatelli.

Scrub the mussel shells and remove the beards with a sharp knife. Discard any that are broken or open. Put them in a pan with the water and cook over a high heat, shaking the pan continuously, until the mussels open. This step only takes about 5 minutes. Discard any mussels that do not open. Remove the mussels from the shells.

Prepare the prawns: remove the head, shell and legs. Most people prefer to leave the tail on. Devein the prawn by removing its digestive tract along the back. Slit open the skin and pull the vein out. Wash thoroughly.

Cook the pasta according to the directions on the packet.

Put the oil in a pan and add the tomato sauce and wine. Cook until the sauce has heated up. Add the mussels and prawns. Keep stirring until the prawns turn pink. Spoon over the drained pasta on individual warm plates. Scatter the basil leaves over the top.

Serves 6–8

Tomato Sauce

2 tablespoons olive oil
1 onion, finely chopped
3 garlic cloves, chopped
1 chilli, finely chopped
1 kg/2¼ lb tomatoes, chopped

39g/1 oz/½ cup basil leaves
Salt and pepper
12 black olives, pitted, optional
Grated Parmesan cheese, to serve

Heat the oil in a saucepan and add the onion. Sauté until the onion is tender but not brown. Add the garlic and a few minutes later the chilli, tomatoes and basil. Season with salt and pepper. Stir well and cook for 10–15 minutes for a fresh-tasting tomato sauce. Add the olives a few minutes before serving, if liked. Serve with any kind of pasta and garnish with Parmesan cheese.
Serves 6

Pesto

Fresh tagliatelle with pesto is one of the most wonderful dishes to start a meal. Pesto is easy to make with a food processor as long as you have a bunch of fresh basil leaves. If you can't get pecorino cheese, use more Parmesan. Pesto can be used as a dip with breads or crudités (p. 11) or a sauce with fish, chicken, beef or lamb.

125g/4 oz/2 cups basil leaves
125 ml/4 fl oz/½ cup virgin olive oil
2 garlic cloves, crushed
2 tablespoons pine nuts (pignolias)
1 teaspoon salt, optional

6 tablespoons freshly grated Parmesan cheese
2 tablespoons freshly grated pecorino cheese
2 tablespoons hot water (preferably pasta cooking water)

Put all the ingredients except the cheeses and hot water into a food processor and blend. Add the cheeses a little at a time. Gradually add the hot water, until it is a smooth, thick paste.
Serves 6

Tomato Sauce is the handiest of all sauces and especially delicious home made.

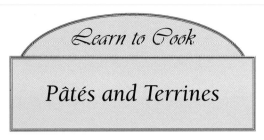

Learn to Cook

Pâtés and Terrines

A pâté or terrine makes an ideal first course, served in individual slices with fresh toast or crusty bread. Tiny cornichons (gherkins) or pickled onions are a traditional accompaniment. 'Pâté' originally meant 'surrounded by pastry'; it was a kind of pie filled with aromatic meats, finely ground or roughly cut. 'Terrine' refers to the earthenware mould the meat is cooked in. It is difficult to make a distinction between pâtés and terrines nowadays.

The meats most commonly used are pork or pork and veal, chicken or game. Fats are included to keep them moist and to bind the meat mixture so it slices well. Flavourings most commonly used are juniper berries, cardamom, allspice, Quatre Epices (p. 34), pepper, salt, thyme, rosemary, bay leaf, garlic, shallots, pistachios, hazelnuts, port, Madeira and table wine.

It is worthwhile buying an attractive terrine dish as it looks wonderful on the table. Make sure the lid fits on tightly.

A thin layer of bacon is usually put on top and around the meat to keep the terrine moist.

Always cook the terrine tightly lidded in a bain marie—that is, place the terrine dish in a baking dish in which there is 2.5 cm/1 inch of hot water. This prevents the terrine from crusting.

To test if the terrine is cooked, insert a skewer—if it comes out clean it is ready.

When the terrine is taken out of the oven, it must be pressed down with a weight while the terrine cools—a can of fruit is usually just right—after first removing the lid of the terrine dish and covering the terrine with greaseproof (waxed) paper. The weight compresses the meats, dispelling any air bubbles that may contain harmful bacteria.

Chill the terrine as soon as it cools and keep it for several days before eating—the flavours continue to mature. The terrine should last up to a week if kept in the refrigerator. Serve at room temperature for the best flavour.

Pâtés and terrines

Combine the ingredients in a bowl and mix well.	*Line a terrine dish with the bacon, leaving the long ends hanging down the side.*	*Press in the meat mixture, cover with bacon and place in a bain-marie. Place lid on terrine.*	*Take terrine from oven, and remove lid. Cover the top with paper and weight it down.*
1	2	3	4

Pâté de Campagne

This is a country pâté, a coarse-textured meat mixture. There are many variations, as anyone who has travelled around the countryside in France knows-every charcuterie seems to have its own variation.

1 kg/2¼ lb/3½ cups minced (ground) pork	2 teaspoons Quatre Epices (p. 34)
175 g/6 oz/1¼ cups bacon, rind removed, finely chopped	2 teaspoons chopped rosemary
2 shallots, finely chopped	2 garlic cloves, chopped
1 teaspoon pepper	2 tablespoons dry white wine
1 teaspoon salt	45 g/1½ oz/⅓ cup pistachio nuts, roughly chopped
	5 bacon rashers (slices), rinds removed

Combine all the ingredients except the bacon in a bowl, mixing well with your hands. Line the terrine dish with the bacon rashers leaving long ends hanging down at the sides to fold over and seal the surface. Press the meat in and arrange the bacon ends over the top. Put the lid on and place the terrine in a bain marie (p. 48). Cook in a preheated oven at 180°C/350°F/gas 4 for ½–2 hours, or until done. Remove from the oven and weight down. Chill when cool.
Makes 8–10 slices

Pork and Veal Terrine

This terrine looks very special when sliced, showing the ham slices in the centre.

1 kg/2¼ lb/ 3½ cups minced (ground) pork and veal	1 egg
2 shallots, finely chopped	1 tablespoon grated lemon peel
1 teaspoon salt	3 tablespoons brandy
2 teaspoons Quatre Epices (p. 34)	125 g/4 oz ham, thickly sliced
1 teaspoon chopped thyme	5 bacon rashers (slices), rinds removed
2 garlic cloves, chopped	

Combine all the ingredients except the ham and bacon. Mix them together well with your hands. Line a terrine dish with the bacon, leaving the long ends hanging down at the sides to fold over the top. Press down half the meat mixture and smooth the surface. Arrange the ham slices over this and put the rest of the meat on top. Smooth the surface and fold the bacon slices over to seal. Put the lid on and place the terrine in the bain marie (p. 48). Cook in a preheated oven at 180°C/350°F/gas 4 for about 1½ –2 hours, or until done. Let it cool with a weight on top and chill.
Makes 8–10 slices

Pork and Veal Terrine served with toasted foccacia, home made pickled onions and cornichorns. Still one of the most flavoursome starters to a meal.

Chicken Pâté

I recommend buying a free-range or corn-fed chicken to get a full-flavoured pâté with this recipe. It really isn't worthwhile going to all this trouble using a battery hen. Remove the pieces of breast before boning and chopping the rest of the chicken.

1 kg/2¼ lb/3½ cups boned and chopped chicken	1 teaspoon salt
500 g/18 oz/3½ cups minced (ground) pork and veal	1 teaspoon chopped tarragon
	4 tablespoons sherry
175 g/6 oz/1¼ cups bacon, rind removed, finely chopped	2 eggs
	225 g/8 oz thick pieces of chicken breast
2 teaspoons Quatre Epices (p. 34)	3 bacon rashers (slices), rinds removed

Combine all the ingredients except for the chicken breast and bacon rashers and mix well. Put one-third of the meat mixture into a terrine dish and smooth the surface. Lay down half the pieces of chicken breast, then cover with another third of the meat mixture. Lay down the other half of the breast pieces and cover with the remaining meat. Smooth the surface and lay the bacon slices on top. Cover the terrine and put in a bain marie (p. 48). Cook in a preheated oven at 180°C/350°F/gas 4 for 2 hours or until done. Test with a skewer. Let the pâté cool with a weight on top and chill.
Makes 10–12 slices

Chicken Liver Pâté

Put this delicious concoction into 4 small porcelain terrine moulds to serve as individual portions with olives and toast or water biscuits (crackers). Serve it preferably the day it is made; if you want to keep it several days, pour a layer of butter over the top after it has cooled, to seal the surface.

90 g/3 oz/6 tablespoons butter
2 shallots, finely chopped
250 g/9 oz chicken livers, trimmed (p. 34)
1 teaspoon finely chopped sage

2 tablespoons brandy
1 teaspoon salt
1 teaspoon pepper
4 bay leaves, to garnish

Melt the butter and cook the shallots until translucent. Add the chicken livers and cook for 3 minutes, stirring continuously. Season with the sage; stir it around to cover and remove from heat. When the livers have cooled, put them into a food processor with any leftover butter. Pour in the brandy, and add the salt and pepper. Blend to a smooth mixture. Pour into the terrine moulds, place a bay leaf on top of each, and chill when cool.
Serves 4

This lovely terrine dish has been placed in a bain-marie, that is, it is sitting in a baking dish of hot water, and is about to go into the oven.

Omelettes

Many different countries have a kind of omelette in their cuisine. The Chinese, Spanish, Italian, Middle Eastern and Indian versions all vary from the classic French omelette.

French Omelettes. A savoury French omelette is a quickly made first course once you have mastered the technique, which does require practice. If you observe the following rules you will find omelettes quite simple to make. The perfect omelette is creamy inside and firm and golden outside.

First you should have a good frying pan (skillet) with a very smooth surface and a heavy base. The heavy base retains the heat better than a thin one, and a non-stick surface is essential so that the omelette doesn't stick to the pan. Some cooks keep a special pan just for omelettes. The pan doesn't need to be larger than 20–23 cm (8–9 inches) for a four-egg omelette which will serve two people. If you are cooking for more, repeat the recipe.

Have all ingredients and equipment ready beside the cooker (stove), because a French omelette must cook quickly over a high heat. An omelette should be eaten as soon as it is cooked, so make sure your diners are ready. Have warm plates ready to serve.

The eggs should be beaten until the yolks and the whites are well blended. Do not pour the eggs into the omelette pan until the butter begins to go slightly brown. This give it a nutty flavour.

The eggs should be at room temperature.

Frittate. The Italian omelette—frittata—is more like a cake and differs greatly from the French. It is cooked slowly over a low heat instead of quickly over a high heat. It is firm and set, not runny inside, and it is kept like a flat open cake, not folded.

Making an omelette

Sauté the sliced mushrooms in a pan until tender.	*In another pan pour in the eggs. Stir so that the eggs cook evenly, then place the mushrooms in the centre.*	*Tilt the pan away from the handle and fold the omelette into an oval shape.*	*Slide the omelette from the pan onto a warm plate.*

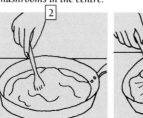
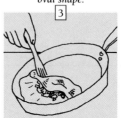
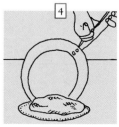

When making a French Omelette shake the pan or stir with a fork to ensure the eggs cook evenly.

A frittata must be cooked on both sides. To do this, it is either flipped over in the pan (or turned over on to a plate and slid back into the pan) or put under the grill (broiler) for a few minutes until the top is cooked.

Fillings for these omelettes are seemingly endless—herbs, cheese, vegetables, meats and seafood.

Serve frittate hot or cold and cut into wedges.

Olive oil may be used instead of butter as the cooking fat.

Eggah. An eggah is a type of omelette popular throughout the Middle East. It bears a close resemblance to the frittata, as it is more like an egg cake but even thicker than the Italian omelette. It is eaten in wedges, hot or cold, and is very popular for picnics and as a first course. Oil or butter may be used as the cooking fat.

Simple French Omelette

Use this technique for the variations that follow. It will serve 2–3 people, so if you are cooking for 4–6, make an extra omelette (in which case you'll need double the quantity of ingredients listed).

5 eggs	¼ teaspoon pepper
¼ teaspoon salt	30 g/1 oz/2 tablespoons butter

An Omelette aux Fines Herbes, a glass of wine and good company—a perfect start to a meal and made in a few minutes.

Beat the eggs with a fork; season with salt and pepper. Melt the butter in an omelette pan. When the butter begins to brown, pour in the eggs. Shake the pan to and fro so that the eggs cook evenly, or stir once or twice with a fork. Tilt the pan away from the handle and, with a fork or spatula, fold the omelette into an oval shape—that is, fold over two sides into the centre. Slide the omelette on to a warm plate with an egg slice, being careful not to break it.

Serves 2–3

Omelette Variations

Mushroom Omelette. Slice 6 mushrooms and sauté them in 15 g/½ oz/1 tablespoon of butter and 1 teaspoon of chopped parsley. When cooked, add them to the egg mixture and proceed to make the omelette. Serves 3.

Omelette aux Fines Herbes. Add 1 tablespoon each of finely chopped parsley, chives, chervil and tarragon to the egg mixture. Serves 3.

Cheese Omelette. Mix 1 tablespoon of grated Gruyère cheese and 1 tablespoon of grated Parmesan cheese to the egg mixture. Serves 3.

Bacon Omelette. Cut 2 bacon slices (rashers), rinds removed, into matchstick pieces. Sauté in butter and when cooked remove with a slotted spoon to the omelette mixture. Proceed to make the omelette at once. Serves 3.

Onion Omelette. Take 2 tablespoons of finely sliced onions and sauté them until they begin to brown. Remove them with a slotted spoon and proceed to make the omelette at once. Serves 3.

Provençale Omelette. Peel, seed and chop 2 tomatoes. Pit 4 black olives and slice finely. Chop 4 basil leaves. Sauté the tomatoes, olives and basil in butter for a few minutes, then add to the egg mixture and make the omelette at once. Serves 3.

Aspagarus Omelette. Cook 3 tablespoons of asparagus tips in water for 5 minutes. Drain and sauté them for a few minutes in butter. Keep warm. Make the omelette in the normal way but place the asparagus in the centre third of the omelette just before you fold over the two sides. *Serves 3.*

Simple Frittata with Cheese

Follow this simple frittata recipe to start, then experiment with the variations.

6 eggs	*125 g/4 oz/1 cup grated Gruyère cheese*
¼ teaspoon salt	*1 teaspoon finely chopped parsley*
½ teaspoon pepper	*45 g/1½ oz/3 tablespoons butter*

Beat the eggs with a fork in a bowl until they are blended. Add the salt, pepper, cheese and parsley and fold them into the eggs. Melt the butter in a 30 cm/12 inch frying pan (skillet) and when it begins to foam, add the egg mixture. Cook over a very low heat. It will take about 15 minutes for the mixture to cook. When it is almost done, finish the top under the grill (broiler) or flip it over to cook the top side. Take the frittata out of the pan with an egg slice. Serve divided into 4
Serves 4

Frittata Variations

Asparagus Frittata. Prepare 225 g/8 oz asparagus, cut into bite-size pieces, in boiling water for 6 minutes. Add them to the egg mixture of the simple frittata and proceed to cook the frittata. *Serves 4.*

Courgette Frittata. Prepare 1 onion, thinly sliced, 3 courgettes (baby marrow, zucchini), thinly sliced, and 1 teaspoon of marjoram. Heat some butter in a pan and sauté the onions and then the courgettes until soft. Add this mixture to the simple frittata recipe and proceed to cook. *Serves 4.*

Broad (Fava) Bean Eggah

A wonderful dish to make in the brief season when broad (fava) beans are available. Otherwise use frozen ones, they are one of the few vegetables that freeze well. Add a chopped chilli if liked.

1 onion, finely sliced	¼ teaspoon pepper
2 tablespoons olive oil	¼ teaspoon salt
6 eggs	1 teaspoon cumin
350 g/12 oz/2 cups broad (fava) beans, cooked	2 tablespoons chopped basil or coriander (cilantro)

Sauté the onion in 1 tablespoon of the oil until it begins to brown. Beat the eggs in a bowl and add the broad beans, onion, pepper, salt, cumin and basil. Mix well. Heat the remaining oil in an omelette pan, and pour in the egg mixture. Turn the heat to low and cook for about 15 minutes. Either flip over as for frittata or place under a grill (broiler) to cook the top. Remove with an egg slice.
Serves 4

Leek Eggah

6 eggs	1 teaspoon salt
800 g/1¾ lb leeks, washed (p. 23)	1 teaspoon pepper
30 g/1 oz/2 tablespoons butter	4 cardamom pods
1 tablespoon lemon juice	2 teaspoons cumin

Beat the eggs in a bowl. Cut the leeks into thin slices and sauté in half the butter. Season with the lemon juice, salt, pepper, cardamom and cumin. Continue to cook until done. Add the leek mixture to the beaten eggs and proceed to make the eggah as for the previous recipe.
Serves 4

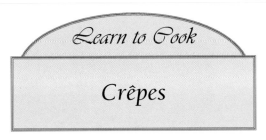

Crêpes

Crêpes can be a savoury dish for the start of a meal or sweetened and eaten as a dessert. They can be made in advance and kept warm or even frozen, to avoid last-minute cooking. They can be served hot or cold, rolled into cylinders around a tasty filling, or folded into triangles.

It is best to buy an 18 cm/7 inch cast-iron crêpe pan and keep it solely for making crêpes. The heavy bottom will distribute the heat evenly; crêpes must be cooked on a high heat and very fast. Do not wash the crêpe pan, just wipe it clean with a paper towel and oil it from time to time.

When freezing crêpes, put a layer of greaseproof (waxed) paper between each pancake and do not stack more than 8–10 at a time.

The savoury fillings can be made from leftovers in the refrigerator, or you can use pasta sauces such as Bolognaise (p. 27), Seafood Sauce (p. 28), Tomato Sauce (p. 30) or Pesto (p. 30), dips such as Guacamole (p. 10), Taramasalata (p. 10) or Smoked Trout Dip (p. 11), or simply a sprinkle of sugar and a squeeze of lemon. Put the sauce in the centre of the pancake and roll it into a cylinder. Serve with melted butter or sprinkled with cheese. Garnish with a lemon wedge or a sprinkling of chopped nuts. At a picnic, roll a cold crêpe around a hot sausage or frankfurter and serve mustard or tomato sauce as extra flavour.

Flip the crêpe over with a spatula and stack when cooked.

Making a crêpe

| Whisk the ingredients together until you have a smooth batter. | Pour the batter into a very hot buttered pan and tilt the pan to get an even surface. | Flip the crêpe over with a egg slice when bubbles begin to appear. | Slide the crêpe from the pan on to the top of the stack of crepes. |

 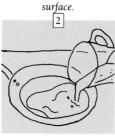 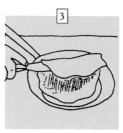 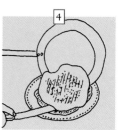

Always let the batter mixture rest for an hour before making the crêpes. It should be very thin; add water if it looks too thick.

Let the butter become a golden brown before adding the batter mixture. This will give it a delicious nutty flavour.

Crêpes are very thin and light, so pour in just a very thin layer of batter. Use as little butter as possible; you may not need to add extra butter to cook each crêpe. Cook them for one minute on each side—flip them over with an egg slice. Transfer the cooked crêpes to a warm plate and keep them warm in a low oven. Stack them as you make them.

Add a tablespoon of caster (superfine) sugar for a sweet crêpe.

Basic Crêpe

125 g/4 oz/1 cup flour, sifted
2 eggs
¼ teaspoon salt

250 ml/8 fl oz/1 cup milk
45 g/1½ oz/3 tablespoons melted butter

Put the flour into a bowl and make a well in the centre. Put in the eggs and salt and one-third of the milk. Mix the egg, salt and milk together with a whisk, then gradually widen the circle to incorporate the flour. Add the rest of the milk and keep whisking until you have a smooth batter. Leave to stand for an hour—it will keep up to 3 days.

Make sure your butter is hot and melted and next to the crêpe pan on the cooker. Heat the crêpe pan and when it is very hot, add a little butter. You need only use enough to prevent the crêpe from sticking—pour off any excess. When it begins to brown, pour in 1½ tablespoons of the batter. Tilt the pan in a circular motion to coat the surface thinly and evenly. When bubbles begin to appear, flip the crêpe over with an egg slice.

Makes about 20

Crêpes with Mushrooms topped with cheese and butter and grilled (broiled) until golden brown.

Crêpes with Mushrooms

Crêpe batter (p. 42)
60 g/2 oz/¼ cup butter
18 mushrooms, sliced
1 tablespoon flour

Salt and pepper
150 ml/¼ pint/ ⅔ cup milk, boiled
125 g/4 oz/1 cup grated Gruyère cheese
½ teaspoon ground coriander seeds

Have the crêpe batter resting. Melt half the butter in a pan and sauté the mushrooms until they are tender. Sprinkle with flour and season with salt and pepper, stirring continuously. Add the milk and half the cheese. Keep warm.

Make 12 crêpes and keep them warm. Put an equal amount of mushroom mixture on to each crêpe and roll the crêpes into cylinders. Place them in a buttered ovenproof dish and sprinkle with the rest of the cheese and butter. Put under a preheated grill (broiler) for about 5 minutes or until the top is golden brown. Serve at once.

Serves 6

Smoked Salmon Crêpes

18 crêpes (see preceding recipe)
300 g/11 oz smoked salmon, thinly sliced

400 ml/14 fl oz/1¾ cups double (heavy) cream
Salt and pepper

Put a slice of salmon in the centre of each crêpe and roll the crêpe into a cylinder. Lay the crêpes in a buttered ovenproof dish and pour the cream over them. Season with salt and pepper. Put under a preheated grill (broiler) to brown the top.

Serves 6

Crêpes with Bacon and Tomato

Crêpe batter (p. 42)
3 tablespoons oil
4 onions, thinly sliced

6 bacon rashers (slices), rinds removed, cut into dice
Salt and pepper
Tomato Sauce, hot (p. 30)

Have the crêpe batter resting. Heat the oil in a saucepan and sauté the onions and bacon until the onions are tender. Season with salt and pepper. Keep warm. Make 12 crêpes and keep them warm. Spread the crêpes with the onion and bacon mixture and roll them into cylinders. Serve on individual heated plates with the tomato sauce poured over one quarter of the surface of the crêpes.

Serves 6

Mushroom Preparation. *Never use any mushrooms that are not fresh, as they may harbour bacteria. Brush them or wipe them with a cloth. If they are field mushrooms and must be washed, be sure to dry them thoroughly. Cut off the untidy end of the stalk but retain the rest of it. When slicing mushrooms, cut them so that you get the attractive shape of the cross-section. Store mushrooms in a ventilated container in the refrigerator.*

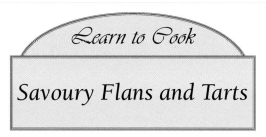

Savoury Flans and Tarts

Don't be daunted by the idea of making your own pastry. Shortcrust pastry (basic pie dough), or pâte brisée, is one of those things that look and taste so wonderful that you think it must be difficult to make, but in fact it is very easy as long as you follow the rules. If you don't have time to make it, use the excellent shortcrust and puff pastry obtainable in supermarkets to make these savoury flans and tarts.

All ingredients should be cool. Shortcrust pastry is made by incorporating butter and flour with just a little cold water to help hold the dough together. It is important that the butter doesn't melt.

The pastry should be mixed with your fingers as quickly and lightly as possible. It doesn't have to be kneaded for long. Just knead it with the palms of your hands until it is smooth. Add more water if necessary to help to bind it.

Chill the pastry for an hour or up to 12 hours in the refrigerator before rolling it out

Bake in a porcelain flan (pie) dish or a metal flan (quiche) ring with a loose bottom—use 20–23 cm/8–9 inch size for these recipes. Lightly grease the flan dish. Roll out the pastry 3 mm/⅛ inch thick. Lift the pastry over the dish or ring and gently ease the pastry into place. Press the pastry into the corners of the ring with your fingertips. Trim off the surplus pastry by rolling your rolling pin along the top. Let the pastry rest for 30 minutes in the refrigerator.

Serve the cooked flan in the porcelain flan dish. Remove the metal flan ring by putting the flan on top of a mug so that the ring drops off the base. Use an egg slice to lift the flan up off the metal bottom and place it on a serving plate.

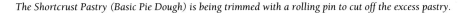

The Shortcrust Pastry (Basic Pie Dough) is being trimmed with a rolling pin to cut off the excess pastry.

Smoked Fish Flan, (p. 47), was made with smoked trout.

Shortcrust Pastry (Basic Pie Dough)

200 g/7 oz/1¾ cups flour, sifted
¼ teaspoon salt
125 g/4 oz/½ cup butter
1 egg yolk

2 teaspoons iced water
Lemon juice
Egg wash (beaten egg yolk)

Sift the flour and salt into a bowl. Cut the butter into small pieces and add to the bowl. Rub the butter into the flour with your fingertips until the butter is completely absorbed and the texture resembles breadcrumbs. Mix the egg yolk with the water and lemon juice. Make a well in the flour, add the liquid and mix together with your fingertips to form a ball. Add more moisture if it gets too dry. Put the dough on a floured surface and knead it lightly with the palms of your hands until it is smooth. Wrap in clingfilm (plastic wrap) and chill for 30 minutes or up to 3 days. (It can also be frozen.) Put the dough on a floured surface and roll it out with a floured rolling pin. Line the flan tin (pie pan) or dish and chill before filling and baking.

Onion Flan

1 quantity Shortcrust Pastry (p. 46)
30 g/1 oz/2 tablespoons butter
1 tablespoon olive oil
4 onions, finely sliced

Salt and pepper
½ teaspoon ground nutmeg
3 egg yolks, beaten
350 ml/12 fl oz/1½ cups single (light) cream

Line a flan tin (pie pan) or dish with the pastry as described in the preceding recipe, and keep refrigerated until the filling is made. Heat the butter and oil in a pan and sauté the onions until soft, about 10 minutes. Remove with a slotted spoon to a bowl. Add the salt, pepper, nutmeg, egg yolks and cream. Mix well. Fill the flan case (pie shell) with the mixture and bake in a pre-heated oven at 190°C/375°F/gas 5 for 30–40 minutes.
Serves 6

Lining a flan tin (pie pan)

| *Knead the dough until smooth and refrigerate to chill. Roll it out.* | *Roll the dough around the rolling pin and transfer it to the flan tin. Unroll over the tin.* | *Push the pastry into the sides of the flan tin and use the roller to cut off excess pastry.* | *If desired, lift round the top edge of the pastry to make a decorative edge.* |

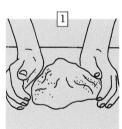
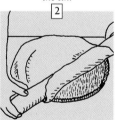
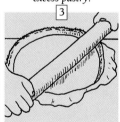
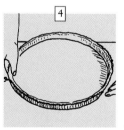

Smoked Fish Flan

Make this with any type of smoked fish, such as haddock, cod or trout. It is absolutely delicious.

1 quantity Shortcrust Pastry (p. 46)
225 g/8 oz cooked and flaked smoked fish
175 ml/6 fl oz/¾ cup double (thick) cream
3 egg yolks, beaten

30 g/1 oz/¼ cup Parmesan cheese
Salt and pepper
1 teaspoon fennel seeds

Line a flan tin (pie pan) or dish with the pastry and chill for 30 minutes. Place the flaked fish in the pastry case (pie shell). Put the rest of the ingredients into a bowl and whisk them together. Pour this mixture over the fish. Bake the flan in a preheated oven at 190°C/375°F/gas 5 for 30–40 minutes.
Serves 6

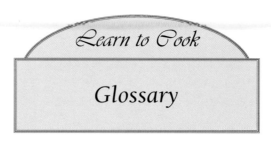

Glossary

Al dente An Italian term referring to the texture of food, meaning almost cooked, just a little firm. Italians like to eat their pasta, rice and vegetables this way.

Bain marie A dish of hot water in which food in a mould or saucepan is stood to cook on top of the hob (stove top) or in the oven. This is to prevent the rapid penetration of heat when cooking, and the steam that surrounds the dish keeps the food moist.

Baste Spoon pan juice over food while it is cooking to keep it from going dry and to crisp the skin.

Bind Hold a food mixture together by adding an egg or liquid.

Blanch Immerse food briefly in boiling water to soften it or to remove skin.

Clarified butter Pure butterfat which will reach a high temperature for frying without burning.

Flake Remove the flesh of the fish carefully from the bones and skin and then pull it apart into smaller bite-size pieces.

Florets Small branch-like pieces of cauliflower or broccoli.

Grissini Thin Italian breadsticks to serve with dips or drinks.

Julienne A French cooking term meaning to cut foods into short, thin strips, like matchsticks, about 5–7.5 cm/2–3 inches long and 3 mm/⅛ inch through (see 'Cutting up Vegetables', p. 15).

Olive oil Extracted from the fruit of the olive tree. The first cold pressing of the olives is the extra virgin oil and the highest quality flavour. Every pressing after that gives lower and lower standards of oil. The better the pressing, the better the flavour. Use the finest quality for salads.

Pitted olives Olives with the stone removed. There are special pieces of kitchen equipment for removing the stones; otherwise use a small knife to prise the olive open to remove the stone.

Refresh Plunge a blanched or cooked food item in to cold water to stop it cooking further.

Roll out Flatten out pasta or pastry dough with a rolling pin into a thin, even sheet.

Sauté Cook briskly in a small quantity of very hot oil, or a mixture of oil and butter, in a large frying pan (skillet). The food is either just browned or cooked through.

Simmer Keep a liquid just below boiling point so that it 'shivers'.

Vinegar Produced by acetic fermentation in wine or cider, it can also be flavoured by herbs, spices, shallots and garlic or raspberries. Balsamic vinegar is an aged vinegar (10–50 years) with a wonderful, delicate flavour.